DEVALUED

Seven Steps to Breaking the Devalue Cycle in Your Life

Meg Torres

TWENTY - SECOND

PUBLISHING

Devalued

7 Steps To Breaking The Devalue Cycle In Your Life

© 2020 by Meg Torres

Printed in the United States of America.

ISBN-13: 978-1-7353705-9-0

Author Photo: Paul Gray Photography

Twenty-Second Publishing

Melbourne, Florida

TWENTY - SECOND
PUBLISHING

ENDORSEMENT

I have known Meg Torres for over twenty-five years. I have served under her leadership and ministered alongside her. In 25 years, Meg has consistently demonstrated the servant-heart of Christ through her limitless compassion for others and her uncompromising integrity. I learned a long time ago – that when Meg speaks, I am well-served to listen. In her quiet, unassuming way, she speaks wisdom and life from the Father's heart. Now that Meg is writing... I know I will be well-served to read!

Pastor Jason Sprinkel

Seneca Assembly of God

This book is dedicated to my husband, Cliff who has valued me every second of every day.

FOREWORD

I have known Meg and her family for ten years. Meg is an amazing woman! She's been a loving wife to Cliff for 25 years, they served as missionaries to Guam (how cool is that!), and she is the proud mom to four children that mean the absolute world to her! Meg has been an educator for 23 years. I was able to see, first hand, how she related to and gave of herself to students so they could achieve success. What is even more impressive is how much the students love and respect her. Meg is a caring friend and someone you can depend on. Meg is a woman of faith and prayer. I am so excited for this new chapter in Meg's life,

I have read many of Meg's writings through the years, and I have always thought she wrote beautifully, so I wasn't surprised when she told me she was writing this book. I was excited and I am telling you....I was hooked in the introduction! Meg will draw you in with her storytelling style. I didn't want it to end!

I have had the pleasure of leading thousands of women through various ministry platforms, and I cannot tell you how many women come to me feeling devalued. Somewhere in their life, they believed the lie that they had no value. They had allowed the words of others to dictate who they were and how they were to feel. The enemy has always been in war against women and he does everything in his power (which is not greater than our God) to devalue us, but we are not going to let him! That cycle ends now in Jesus' name.

There are amazing scriptures that will lift you up and speak life into you. This book in your hands is another marvelous tool that will help you heal and grow, if you let it.

You have been created by God. You have been created with a purpose. You are not a mistake! You are fearfully and wonderfully made. You are God's marvelous masterpiece. Matthew 10:31 says, "So do not fear, you are more valuable than many sparrows."

Get your highlighter in your hand and keep a journal close by because you will have a lot to learn, meditate on, apply, and grow from these 7 Steps to Breaking the Cycle of Devalue in Your Life.

Sorines Lopez

Author of 7 Actions of a Wise Woman

Contents

Introduction

I had five minutes before my fourth grade class came bursting through the door from recess. I quickly picked up the small pieces of trash on the floor; a crumpled piece of paper, a broken off pink eraser, a flattened paper clip, a bread bag tie, a sticker, a fruit snack, and a feather. I laughed to myself at the array of items my very energetic class of fourteen had managed to discard in just a few hours. As I deposited their trash into the trashcan and thought about how I could once again reword the lecture I would give them about taking care of our classroom, I heard the low mutterings of their return as they tried to heed the directions to be quiet in the hall. I opened the door and welcomed them back, each by name, the scent of sweat and dirt swirling with the smell of the cherry lip gloss Macy had brought to share with all the girls.

As they took their seats, I opened the chapter book we were reading together as a class. The custodian came in and took the trash as he always did early afternoon. His arrival reminded me of the impending lecture I needed to give about keeping our classroom clean. As I was reading the next chapter in our book, Michael raised his hand. The students knew that they needed to wait until I was done for questions, so I read on, ignoring his raised hand. As often happens, the hand began to shake and wave and wiggle, trying to get me to break my own rule, but I stood firm in my pursuit to keep law and order. The wiggling hand was soon accompanied by a low whine, which increased in tone and volume. This was uncharacteristic for Michael. His classmate, the ever-present, dazzling, cherry lip-glossed Macy, whispered to him, and Michael responded. I read on in all my teacher glory, proud of my ability to follow my own rule. Though I was bound to my rules, Macy was not. She said, "Mrs. Torres. This is an emergency. Michael's special, special item is missing. Someone stole it."

It is important to take a minute to talk about Macy. Fact one: Every morning, Macy came in either crying, on the verge of tears, or with a red, blotchy face, having just finished crying. Mornings were rough for her. Mom was not the best in the morning, so Macy had to get up, get her siblings up, and get everyone ready. She had to make breakfast and pack lunches and get her mom up to drive them to school. She was always late. Every. Single. Day. At the beginning of the school year, I was frustrated every morning because one thing about Macy, she could not enter quietly or subtly or inconspicuously. Most mornings, Macy pushed the door open with her foot, backpack unzipped, items falling to the group. She would simultaneously try to enter the room and pick up what had fallen, dropping even more items. She was always out of breath because she had run from the entrance of the school to the classroom. Many times, she was openly sobbing. She knew how to make an entrance. After multiple attempts to call Mom and talk to her about tardies and the consequences associated with them, I realized it was not going to change. Fact two: Macy never had her homework done. Afternoons were not really Mom's thing either. Macy often had to call her mom because Mom was late picking her up. When she got home, she and her siblings were told to play outside until dark. No one was helping her with her homework. This made Macy sad. When I would call for homework to be turned in, she would sit in her seat, usually the only one, defeated. Fact three: Macy was never absent. She came to school, rain or shine, sick or well, hungry or full. She would even show up on teacher workdays when the students had a day off from school.

Once I realized that her arriving to school on time was not an option, I knew that we had to come up with a way to rebuild Macy every morning. Three friends were assigned to help her when she arrived; one to take her backpack, zip it up, and put it in the cubby; another to walk her to her seat and get her tissues; and a third to catch her up on where we were in our lesson. Macy also needed time to vent about her morning. Once she was seated, I would ask her how she was and she would tell us, no holds barred. Yes, students would roll their eyes and get frustrated. It was time-consuming and nerve-racking, but it was necessary. Macy came to us having been devalued and broken down. We made it our mission to build her up.

If Macy had to be described by the education system, we would say that she was at-risk, unorganized, habitually tardy, lacked parental guidance, prone to discipline issues, and in need of education interventions. However, what the educational system could not see and would never list in their description of Macy was the most significant thing about her. She possessed a keen, supernatural insight to see anyone or anything (she was forever saving hurt bugs and returning worms to their proper habitat) that was hurting and to come to the rescue. This is what she was doing with Michael, coming to his rescue by reporting that someone had stolen his special, special item.

I smiled. Why do they always go straight to the thought that someone stole it? I stopped my reading and asked Michael what his special item was. He said, "It's one of those plastic pieces that keeps the bread bag closed." I informed Michael that it was on the floor, and I had thrown it out. To this, he responded with a gut-wrenching howl and slid off his chair onto the ground, the tears flowing. I had never known Michael to break a rule, to cry, or in any other way draw attention to himself. I walked over to him and helped him up, the sobbing continued. He was inconsolable. His classmates surrounded him, offering tissues and water bottles and back pats and hugs.

We had a place in the classroom called the Community Corner, where we would go the last ten minutes of the day and discuss anything that happened that day that we needed to get off our chests. Since the inception of the Community Corner, tattling had been reduced greatly. I told the class that we were going to change our schedule and go to the Community Corner so we could help Michael feel better. As we sat, I asked Michael why the bread tie was so special to him. He said that every Saturday, his grandpa who lives with him and his mom, would get up with Michael and they would make toast. His grandpa would twirl the bag in the air and remove the bread tie, then put the toast in the toaster at a setting of six; browned but not burned, crispy but still soft in the middle. Then his grandpa would put jelly on the toast and the type of jelly would always be a surprise for Michael. Michael told us that he loved grape the most but would eat whatever his grandpa picked. He then shared that three months ago, his grandpa got up for their toast-making breakfast and realized the jelly was gone. While Michael got everything ready, his grandpa went to the store just one street away for jelly. His grandpa was in a car accident on the way back from the store and died. Ever since, Michael had kept the bread tie with him at all times.

Tears were abundant in the Community Corner. One student told him that his grandpa died too, and another offered to make a bread tie for him in art class. As for me, I was heartbroken. I had thrown away his special, special item. I had picked it up, and without hesitation, classified it as trash. What had I done? Macy spoke up and said, "Mrs. Torres, we have to go get it right now." Everyone agreed, and before I could respond, they had formed a line at the door with Michael in the middle, both of his hands being held, one from his friend in front of him and the other from his friend behind him. It made walking in a line awkward, but they were not letting go.

We found the custodian who told us that he had taken the trash to the dumpster. I could see all hope was lost on all faces, except for sweet Macy. She pointed to the sky, and with all the vim and vigor that accompanies the confidence of cherry lip gloss, shouted, "To the dumpster!"

It is important to note that there is a significant confidence that comes with cherry lip gloss. As a little girl, I remember wanting to wear my mom's make-up. She always looked stunning, and though I could occasionally try some on, I could not wear it in public. I was too young. Lip gloss, however, was the bridge between the world of childhood and the world of pre-teen. Lip gloss was not really make-up, but it wasn't nothing. I remember when I could choose my own lip gloss, right around the same age as Macy. The lip gloss came in little cylinder glass bottles. The choices were bubble gum, cotton candy, watermelon, grape, and of course, cherry. There was something about cherry. It had a slight red tint to it and smelled delicious. As a fourth grader, when applied, you felt a certain kind of way; and as an adult, a good application of lip gloss can bring back memories of that childhood confidence. The value of cherry lip gloss was not lost on me. I had given Macy the lip gloss as a prize for going an entire day without interrupting. I saw her face change and her eyes light up when she put it on and ran to the bathroom to see herself in the mirror. Inside her emotions, she carried hurts and scars. Inside her head, she carried the words of adults who told her she was stupid and ugly, but deep inside her heart, she carried the strength to bear another's burdens, and her cherry lip gloss gave her the extra boost of confidence to lead her classmates.

Without prompting, the entire class responded, "To the dumpster!" We went outside and arrived at the dumpster, filled to the brim. Lunch had ended and the cafeteria trash had been deposited. Bags filled with Hot Pockets wrappers, sandwich crusts, discarded fruit, small milk cartons, and the combination of liquids the third graders had mixed together in a Styrofoam cup. I removed the cafeteria bags to get to the smaller white trash bags that come from classrooms. I opened the first one, I could see from its contents that it was not from my classroom. The next bag was definitely from the science lab. It was dissection day. I looked in the third, fourth, and fifth bag to no avail. I could not reach the other bags. I looked at Macy for support and she said, "Ok guys, she's going in." I climbed in and found our bag; our bag filled with trash but containing one special, special treasure. I ripped it open, and the students spilled it onto the grass and found the bread tie. There were more tears and cheering and clapping and some of those little girls squealy, jumping circles.

Michael let go of his friends' hands for the first time since our journey began, and received the bread tie from Macy. She spoke for all of us when she said, "We're sorry. We didn't know it was valuable."

Believe it or not, "valuable" had been one of our vocabulary words that week, and as Macy made her statement, I started to think of the sentences that had accompanied the word in our daily vocabulary lesson; sentences like, "my mom's ring is very valuable," "gold is a valuable mineral," and "one hundred dollars is more valuable than twenty dollars." I realized at that moment that the students had been directed to use the word to accompany the value found in things, in material objects, in monetary ways. However, what they showed me was that they understood the meaning of the word when it came to the human spirit, when it came to a small human, just about their size, who slid off his chair and cried out in anguish. They understood that he was valuable. His pain was valuable. He was valuable enough to be handed tissue, to be hugged, for his hands to be held, and for a class trip to the dirty, smelly dumpster.

We kept the word "valuable" as part of our vocabulary list every week for the rest of the year, and we always wrote sentences that spoke of the value of people, the value of a soul, the value of one human life. Learning that we are valuable starts with understanding that we were made in the image of God and that our value is assigned by Him and Him alone. There are so many things that will attempt to rob us of our value, but God wants us to accept our value, understand our value, and use our value to build up others. And let's not forget Macy, oh Macy, the one who struggled the most, the one who was pushed aside every morning and every evening, the one who felt more pain than most of her classmates; she was the one who led the charge. Perhaps she understood the significance of being valued more than anyone else because she was coming from a place of being devalued. Being devalued affects every area of our lives, from our spirits to our minds, to our bodies, to our dreams, to our relationships. There are seven steps we can take to move from a place of devalue to a place of value.

Chapter One

Step One - Understanding Value vs. Devalue

In order to really understand what value and devalue are, we need to dive into the meanings of the words themselves. The English word *value* is from the Latin word *valere*, which means "ability, utility, and importance." The word *valuable* in Scripture is derived from the Hebrew word *yâqâr*, which has several meanings, including "valuable, prized, weighty, precious, rare and splendid." *Devalue* means "to reduce or underestimate the worth or importance of." When we look at the synonyms for the word *devalue*, we grasp even more what the meaning is. Common synonyms for *devalue* are "belittle, depreciate, disparage, denigrate, make light of, treat lightly, discredit, underrate, and undervalue." How value is assigned to something is based on several factors, including culture and upbringing.

Culture has a great impact on value. I have been in other countries and have experienced value in the context of other cultures. When I was in Equatorial Guinea, Africa, I went to my first church service the day after I arrived. When the pastor called for the offering, everyone started clapping, singing, and dancing their way to the front. Few had money, but there was an abundance laid at the front; live chickens, cloth, vegetables, a bowl, and even a neatly tied together pile of sticks. I was the only one in my seat because I had no money, so I thought I had no offering. In my culture, the value was placed on the gift; in their culture, it was placed on the giver. When I was in Costa Rica, we went to a village to paint a church building. When we came, we brought rice, beans, and other food items for the people of the village. As we finished painting, we were brought a meal of rice and beans and tortillas and goat cheese. I was hesitant to accept it because I knew their need for food was great, but they insisted and were happy to give. In my culture, the value was placed on the items of provision; in their culture, the value was placed on the provider. In another village in Africa, I saw a village woman give birth to a child, and within a few hours, the baby was strapped to her back, and she was out cutting down sugar cane with a machete. All the while, her husband was in the bush with the other men, drinking and telling stories. I was upset by this, but it was explained to me the sugar cane was harvested by the women and brought to the men to sell. It was a place of honor for the women to provide both children and sugar cane for their husbands. In my culture, the value was placed on rest for a woman who has just given birth; in their culture, the value was placed on work in spite of having given birth.

Western culture can be confusing when it comes to how culture contributes to value. I am at that middle stage of life where I can look back on my childhood and remember what our culture was like then, and at the same time, I am raising teenagers who are experiencing a whole other culture. When I was growing up, I hated my eyebrows. I should say eyebrow because I had one big unibrow. I would compare my eyebrows to my friends and see some that were like mine and others that were not like mine. Now, if a teenage girl does not like her eyebrows, she can browse through thousands of pictures and watch hundreds of tutorials on eyebrows. She can read articles on eyebrows and see pictures of girls who have the wrong eyebrows according to cultural trends. The value that I, as a teenager, and my culture at that time, placed on eyebrows, was minimal. I did not have much to compare them to. The value placed on eyebrows now, in our culture, is exponential because there are so many types, so many products, and so many ways to feel not good enough by your eyebrows alone. Social media and the internet bombard us with ideas concerning cultural trends, and value is tied to following those trends. Whether or not we accept it, culture dictates to us value on many levels.

I could go further and share so many stories of the way I have seen value within cultural settings However, the point is that culture contributes to value, and when it comes to the value of the human spirit and a human life, culture plays a role as well. You can go to the internet and find just as many stories, examples, videos, and rants valuing life as you can devaluing life. I can search for videos of puppies being rescued and puppies being tortured. I can search for videos about teenagers being built up and videos of teenagers being sold. I can search and find videos of the elderly being honored and videos of the elderly being abused. When we live in a culture that sends mixed signals about value, it can be hard to find our way. We have to acknowledge that our culture influences value.

The way we are raised greatly contributes to our idea of value as well. When we are growing up, we focus on our small world and what our immediate family shows to be valuable. Something valued in my house growing up were holidays. Every Easter, my brothers and I had huge overflowing baskets with special chocolates from a local candy store in the shape of things we loved. I would get a ballet dancer or flower. My brothers would get footballs or teddy bears. Every Valentine's Day, I would receive a heart filled with candy from my dad. Every Christmas was filled with stockings stuffed to the brim and presents under the tree. We would decorate together; make homemade fudge and peanut butter blossom cookies. As I started to make friends in school and was exposed to what they valued, I found out that things were different. One of my friends got an orange and a pair of pantyhose in her stocking every year. I thought it was awful, but she told me a story about how that came to be their tradition, and it was unique and special to her family. More important than the value placed on events or material things growing up is the value placed on the human spirit. Did you have parents who yelled at each other and said demeaning things or parents who loved each other and spoke highly of one another? Were you yelled at for doing wrong or instructed in how to learn from your mistakes in order to do better? Were you told often that you were loved, special, and a gift, or were you told you were a mistake, stupid, or not wanted? These words have incredible impact on how we understand value.

Here is where devaluing comes into play. When value is assigned along the backdrop of culture and upbringing, we are led either on a path of value or a path of devalue. However, at any point along our journey, an incident, a word, an experience, or a thought pattern can cause us to switch the path we are on. Every person experiences a mixture of value and devalue along their path, and a series of events or decisions can lead in one direction or another. I was raised in a home where I always felt valued by my parents. I heard often that I was loved and I was special and I was smart. However, unknowing to my parents, I had another family member who devalued me, called me names, abused me, and broke me. I also felt that peace and lack of confrontation were valued in my home. This, along with my personality, caused me not to speak about what was happening to me. I was raised knowing I was valued while having devaluing experiences. So as I became a teenager, I, like Macy, had a keen sense to see who around me was devalued and dejected, and how to lift them up; yet I did not see that I myself was on a path of devalue.

Sometimes we can trace our acceptance of being devalued to a specific time or event or experience, while other times, we cannot. We all encounter moments where we are valued and moments where we are devalued. When it comes to understanding the cycle of devalue or the pattern of being valued, we have to ask ourselves some questions that go back to the meaning of the words *value* and *devalue*. Ask yourself the following questions. Your answers could refer to your job, marriage, a ministry, a family relationship, a friendship, or even how you treat yourself: Are you appreciated? Are you esteemed? Esteemed means to be held in high respect. Are you held dear? This means you are treasured and cared for. Is your worth expressed? Are you important? Are you prized? Are you admired? Are you cherished? Answering yes to these questions shows a pattern of being valued. Maybe you can answer yes for one area of your life but no in another area. Now consider these questions: Do you find yourself in situations where you are belittled? We tend to think of belittling as being talked down to, but belittling is as simple as being talked about in a way that makes you less important than you are. Are you depreciated? Depreciated is usually applied to materialistic thoughts. A car depreciates in value over time, for example. However, people can be depreciated as well. Depreciated means to lower in honor or esteem. Were you initially honored in your marriage or esteemed in your job, but over time, that has changed to a lack of appreciation? Have you experienced disparage? The definition of *disparage* is telling. To disparage someone is a "specific way to describe a certain kind of insult, the kind that secures the insulter's place as superior. It often refers to an opinion or criticism lobbed in print or via word of mouth, not necessarily an act done to someone's face." Are you being denigrated? *Denigrate* comes from the Latin verb *denigrare*, which means "to blacken," and is used to mean "criticized unfairly or to blacken someone's reputation." Are you made light of or treated lightly? This refers to not being taken seriously, when in fact, what you are saying is serious. Are you underrated? To be underrated means you do not receive the merit, recognition, or praise you deserve. Are you undervalued? Being undervalued means not recognizing how important or valued someone is. Answering yes to these questions shows a cycle of devalue. As was stated with value, you could answer yes to these questions in one area and no in another.

When answering these questions, we want to make sure we do not have a false sense of pride or entitlement. There are times at a job where we do something without recognition, and that is reasonable. There are times in marriage where we do not value our spouse like we should. There are moments where we get caught up in the business of life, and our friendships lose value. There may be a time, once a year, where you feel unappreciated at your job. I am not talking about these moments. I am talking about a cycle of devalue or a pattern of value, where you can answer yes to these questions for a significant amount of time in a specific area (job, marriage, relationship, etc.). These are legitimate questions that will help determine patterns in devaluing or valuing relationships. Now that we have laid the foundation for understanding value and devalue, let's look at the tactics that are used by people who devalue others. I call them Devaluers.

Chapter 2:

Step 2 - Understanding the Three Ds of Devaluers

Not all Devaluers know they are Devaluers, but in my experience, they tend to use similar tactics. Being devalued looks different as a child, teenager, and adult. A child may struggle to understand what is happening, having a feeling something is not right. A child may look at others around them and try to figure out if what is happening to them is normal. Is it happening to a classmate? What do I hear when I go to a friend's house? How do other parents treat their children at the grocery store? Of course, a child has little control over what is happening. Children are not mature enough to process the emotions of it. A teenager who is being devalued will understand on some level that it is wrong. It can be as simple as thinking, "she shouldn't talk to me that way" or "he said he was only joking, but he keeps doing it over and over" or "why does she talk to me like I am stupid all the time?" An adult who is being devalued is often so far into the cycle that it becomes normal. We have all heard people talk about sabotaging a good relationship or friendship. I used to never understand that, but the more I have learned about the behavior that accompanies years of being devalued, I understand that the devaluing becomes normal, and when a true relationship of value comes along, the devalued do not know how to be valued.

As I was coming out of my abuse at the hands of a family member, I found myself in relationships with others who continued to devalue me in other ways. Though I had many healthy relationships and friendships, there was still a piece of me that was attracted to Devaluers. I did not yet understand the root of why I accepted this kind of treatment. I had a friend who would invite me over, and even though I knew without a doubt that I would be treated poorly, I would go to her house. She would do things, like have me go outside to see the snowfall and then lock me out of the house in the cold with no coat. She would make me food, but secretly put spices in it that would burn my mouth. She would offer me her clothes to wear, knowing they were too small, and then nag me over and over to try them on just to gloat that they did not fit. In this lies the first tactic of a Devaluer. Devaluers are demeaning. To demean someone is to put someone down or lower them by doing something that harms their pride. In my situation, the demeaning would sting twice. When my friend would invite others over, she would tell them the stories. "You guys should have seen Meg trying to fit into my jeans. She was laying on the bed and I was trying my hardest to zip them. I even used a hanger to try and pull up the zipper, but it wouldn't work." She would laugh and I would smile. I was sure to always act as if it was fine; always keeping peace, always avoiding conflict. Those being devalued remain quiet and keep the peace because there must be a level of value to believe your words will make a difference. When you are being devalued, you are convinced that your words are meaningless. By demeaning people, Devaluers know they have the upper hand. They know that there are no words that can restore the pride that they took away.

When I was in high school, I started dating what I consider to be my first real boyfriend. He was cute and cool. I was shy and not good at talking to people I did not know, but I had a best friend who was more than willing to talk for me. She let him know that I thought he was cute and gave him my number. He called a few times that week and we talked. Well, actually, he talked and I listened. He talked about himself, a lot. He ended our third conversation by saying, "I don't really want to ask you out, but I feel like God is making me, so will you be my girlfriend?" Now, at this moment, if I had understood my value, I would have understood what was to come should I accept his offer and said no, but being in a state of devalue, I said yes. Throughout the time we dated, it went something like this: I wouldn't hear from him for several days, then go to hang out with a group of friends, and he would be there, acting like he hadn't ignored me for days. He would then show up at my house a few days later with friends in the car to say hi, but tell me he couldn't stay because he had plans. He would call me at random times to see if I wanted to hang out, and when he picked me up, I would ask where he had been or why he hadn't called. He would say he was busy or he was working. One time, he called me to say he was coming to pick me up. When I got out to the car, there was a girl in the front seat. I got in the back, and he introduced us. We drove around and then went to his house to hang out. When we went into his living room, he sat on the couch. As I moved to sit next to him, so did the girl from the car who boldly took the seat. I sat in a chair. When his mom came home, she called for him to come help her with groceries. When he left the room, car girl asked me how long he and I had been friends. I said, "I'm not his friend, I'm his girlfriend." She told me that I must have misunderstood how he felt about me because she was his girlfriend. He had asked her out the night before. He came back into the room with his family, so our conversation ended. When it was time to go, I willingly got into the backseat, the whole time questioning if I had misunderstood the past nine months. Had I done something wrong? He dropped her off first. She actually gave him a kiss as she got out of the car. You may be reading this and think you know what came next, that I broke up with him, walked away, and never looked back. I wish I had done that, but instead, I listened to his explanation. He had gone to a party with some friends and drank a little. He ended up accidentally asking the girl out. I mustered up the courage to say that I did not think it was right and that I was hurt. He then said, "Come on, it's not a big deal, right? She's nice and doesn't go to church. I don't want to make her feel bad. I don't know why you are upset." And then he told me that I couldn't be hurt because there was no such thing as feelings. Herein lies the second tactic of the Devaluer, and that is dismissing. When someone dismisses you, they decide or say that you are not important enough for them to think about or consider. When someone dismisses you, they are rejecting you and disregarding you. My boyfriend's behavior continued. I was dismissed at every turn; ignored, and embarrassed, but somehow, I continued on, trying to be what he needed, even if it was a doormat to wipe his grimy shoes on. When we think of dismissal or rejection, we think of the end of something, but if you have been in this type of devaluing relationship, you know the heartbreak of being dismissed and rejected continually while staying in the relationship. Devaluers who use this tactic take what little voice remains inside of you and silence it. They take the smallest spark of value that may be hanging on and extinguish it for good.

My first job was babysitting for a family. The mom was so wonderful to me. She would order me pizza or get my favorite fast food. She would rent movies for me to watch when the kids fell asleep. She bought me Christmas presents. She always asked me about my life and my friends. After that, I worked in a locally owned Christian bookstore. The owner and his wife were amazing people who treated me well. They recognized my abilities, even at the age of 14, and continually encouraged me and trained me to do even more within their little company.

One summer, I even had a job shoveling dehydrated poultry manure. The job was not glamorous, but the boss spoke to me every day and thanked me for a job well done. These are the types of employers we all hope to have; employers who value their workers, whether they are managing their business or shoveling manure. Unfortunately, not all employers value their employees. There are times when bosses, employers, and leaders are Devaluers.

Being devalued at work is an especially precarious situation. Many times, individuals love what they do at their job, but are devalued and need to make a difficult choice. I have spoken to people who are frustrated with how they are treated at work, and they say things like, "well at least I'm getting paid" or "it's just her management style" or "I probably can't find another job so I will just stay." Those are all statements made by people who have been devalued at work. I want to be sure that we distinguish between being devalued at work and being dissatisfied at work. When we become dissatisfied in a job, we can become cynical or overly critical. Dissatisfaction is a time for reflection and asking if it is time to look for another job, or ask for a raise, or seek out additional education. We have all had bosses we do not particularly like or employers who are challenging to work for. No work environment is perfect. This is different from being devalued.

While in college, I got a job at a large organization. I was so excited to work there even though it was only a six-month temporary job. I was hired to assist the editor of a monthly magazine. When I arrived, I was given a desk and a computer. The editor met with me and said I would be answering the phones, making phone calls, and contacting writers about deadlines for the magazine. I did this for a couple of weeks, then the editor left, taking a job in another department. I was told just to answer the phones and take messages until they hired someone. I answered the phone, but the calls began to be about deadlines, and production, and printing, and photos for articles. I began to make decisions the best I could, answer questions in the way I thought would be best, and the magazine was released. When it came out, the head boss of the department came to ask me how the magazine was completed and released. I told him that I figured out how to do what needed to be done and made it happen. He said, "Great, do that again." The next month's magazine was already in the works, so I continued doing the editor's job, happy to be recognized by the head boss. After doing this two more months, I felt I had more than proven myself. I had taught myself layout software, production, and story editing. So, I set up a meeting with the head boss. I had planned my speech and practiced it all morning. I had even brought the magazines with me to use as examples. In my meeting, I told him that I had produced three magazines with no training or assistance and would like to continue as the editor. I suggested that I get paid the editor's salary instead of the small temp salary I was working for. He asked me who had told me to do what I was doing. I told him that he had. I recounted our conversation when he came to find out how the magazine had been completed. He told me that I was never specifically told to do what I was doing, so I should not have been doing it. I asked if there was a problem with the magazine and he said, "No, it's great." I said that I did not think it was fair that I did the work and did not get the pay. He said that he didn't think it was fair that I did a job that I was not qualified for when there were people in the building who might like that job. He then asked my educational qualifications to be an editor. I told him that I was still in college and I did not have specific educational qualifications, but three months of publishing the magazine should show that I am qualified. He told me that college students are temp employees and many of the college students in town would love to work there. I should be happy with my temp position. Then he concluded our meeting by saying, "Thanks for being willing to meet with me today." Wait…hadn't I scheduled the meeting? He continued, "I am glad you like working here and want to continue as a temp employee." Hadn't I just said that I didn't want to continue as a temp employee? And finally, "I'm sorry you don't feel you have the qualifications to be an editor. Maybe check back in the future." Wait…hadn't I said that I did feel I had the qualifications? I am not sure if he had a special button under his desk that summoned his secretary, but she magically appeared at this point to walk me out. Herein lies the third tactic of Devaluers, and that is deflecting. Deflecting is to deter someone from his or her intended purpose, to change the subject, to get someone to change what they are talking about, to intensely focus on the other person's actions and behaviors so the attention is taken off of you. When a Devaluer deflects, in a sense, they turn the tables on you. You come to them with legitimate concerns, and instead of hearing the concerns and talking about them, they turn the tables by saying, "What about you?" In a relationship, it may look like this. You tell your spouse that they hurt your feelings when they did not answer your phone calls. They respond by listing all the times you did not answer their phone calls and throw in all the times you did not answer their texts. They go back to three years ago when you were dating, and they came to your apartment, and you did not answer the door. A little bit of deflection is normal for all of us. No one likes to take the blame for something or to be accused, and sometimes our response is to deflect in some way. However, when it comes to Devaluers, every conversation you have with them that goes beyond small talk and common day-to-day conversation ends in deflection. By deflecting, the Devaluer leaves you feeling like you did something wrong, you are the one at fault, and you should not bring it up again because you will look stupid. The Devaluer is left feeling justified in their actions. In this particular job, I received a notice a week later that an editor had been hired and I would be moved to another temp position…after I trained the editor.

It is time to ask yourself some questions: Do you find yourself in a relationship, friendship, or job where you are demeaned? Are you put down or made lower by comments or actions? Is your pride continually hurt through humiliating situations? Do you find yourself in a relationship, friendship, or job where you are dismissed? Are your words and thoughts not even important enough for the other person to think about or consider? Are you continually rejected? Are you disregarded? Do you find yourself in a relationship, friendship, or job where your legitimate concerns are deflected? When you try to speak about important things or your feelings, are your past actions brought up so the attention is put on you? If you answered yes to some or all of these questions, you are most likely in a situation with a Devaluer. That is where I found myself when I went to college.

I attended college in the early 1990s. It was the first time I had really been away from home. The drive from New York to Missouri was long, and saying goodbye to my mom was heartbreaking. I was not sure I would make it, but I quickly made some good friends and started experiencing college life. Eventually, I met a young man that was charismatic and handsome. He was popular and always laughing and smiling. Everyone knew his name. Everyone said hi when he walked by. I was a shy, timid, introverted girl who was sure he would never look my way. To my surprise, through a series of events, he ended up asking me out and we started dating. Pretty soon into our relationship I learned that he didn't really care about me. He cared about himself and how others saw him, but it was okay with me. I was an expert in dating the wrong type of guy, and I knew how to stay in a relationship where I was not important. I knew the rules: Be quiet. Laugh at his jokes. Do not ask for anything. Do not bring up your feelings. You are there for him. Let him lead the conversation. Do not call if he does not call you, no matter how many days go by. Do not mention him flirting with other girls. Accept the insults as jokes. Expect to be treated worse in front of his friends. Do not bring him around your friends. Build him up while he tears you down.

One night, we were going on a date. I met him in the lobby of his dorm, and we were sitting on a couch while he tied his shoes. There was no one else in the lobby except one other student sitting in an armed chair nearby. Some of my boyfriend's friends came through the lobby and asked what we were doing. He said that we were going out to eat and they asked where. He said, "I don't know. Somewhere with a buffet, so Meg can just pull up a chair and eat. It's cheaper that way." He laughed. They laughed. I laughed. But inside, I was humiliated. I was embarrassed. I could feel the heat in my cheeks and the sting behind my eyes, but I smiled and recited the rules of our relationship in my head. As his friends left, he got up to go get his wallet and gave me a kind of pat on the back. This pat was given often. It was like him saying, "Good job. You did your part. You smiled. You let my friends laugh at you. Good girl."

I was relieved to sit in silence. I was relieved that it was only his friends who heard the remark. I tucked my hair behind my ear, a nervous habit, and tried to sink into myself. Out of the corner of my eye, I saw the student who was sitting in the armchair nearby. I had forgotten he was there. We made eye contact and he said, "What are you doing with him? You deserve better than that." With that, he got up and left. To this day, I remember that moment so clearly. A total stranger had heard the comment, had seen the treatment, had picked up on my fake laugh, had somehow sensed the rules of our relationship, and called my bluff. The question played over in my mind, "What are you doing with him?" I could not answer it because I did not know. This was the first step in me realizing what it looks like to be devalued. It was the first step in me recognizing that maybe I did deserve something more. Now that we can recognize the tactics of a Devaluer, we need to understand why we stay in a place of devalue.

Chapter 3

Step 3 - Understanding Why We Stay in a Place of Devalue

By now, you should have a firm understanding devaluing is and a good idea of what situations you are in that are devaluing. Now we need to ask: why do we stay in devaluing situations? What makes us accept this type of treatment? When I read over my descriptions of my devaluing relationships, I cringe. I cringe at the woman that I was. Putting it into words and opening up the parts of my life where I struggled so deeply to find value is vulnerable. However, it is worth it to help bring healing to anyone who is stuck in a devaluing relationship or job or even church. Answering the "why" is important. The "why" is often different for each person, yet there are common threads that I have noticed as I have talked to individuals who are in a cycle of devalue.

Sometime after college, I found myself in a job with a leadership role. I worked very hard and was proud of the work. I was often told to complete assignments and do tasks by my direct supervisor. My direct supervisor and I had a good working relationship. I was valued for my experience, expertise, and knowledge; however, the workload was all-consuming. I worked hours in the evenings and weekends to complete tasks. If I told my supervisor that I was overwhelmed, my supervisor would take on some of the work, adding to the already full plate in their hands. I would do the same for those below me. No one in upper management acknowledged our hard work. If we were to say that our workload was too big, we were told that we did not have good time management skills or we did not delegate well (deflecting). If we heard of an issue that everyone in the organization was having and brought it to upper management, we were told it wasn't really a problem, and everyone needed to work it out themselves (dismissing). If a mistake was made or something fell through the cracks because of the overwhelming amount of work, we were reprimanded for dropping the ball often before we could even explain the what or why of the situation. This reprimanding tended to be in a way that involved feeling intimidated or in danger of losing our job (demeaning). So why did I stay at this job for some time? Because I was a buffer. I valued those who worked under my leadership and those who worked directly above me, and they valued me. If I could serve as a buffer to keep them from experiencing the devalue I was experiencing, I was willing to do so. This happens regularly. How often does a parent stay in a devaluing relationship to be the buffer between the Devaluer and the children? How often does a person stay with a devaluing friendship because they are the buffer between the Devaluer and the other friends in the group? How often does someone refuse to acknowledge or discuss Devaluing behavior from a parent because they are the buffer between parent and siblings? We need to accept that being a buffer is not healthy for us or for those we are being a buffer for. And here is why, in being a buffer, you are taking on an emotional role in hopes that either side will see how caring and protective you are, thus assign value to you. You cannot receive the value you crave by taking on the devalue meant for those around you. Being a buffer only adds to your feelings of devalue.

I was recently with a friend, and while we were talking, her phone was getting text message after text message. Though she was trying to be polite, it was clear the texts needed to be acknowledged. She explained that the texts were from a friend who was upset with her. My friend told me that they had been friends for over ten years. She said when they were first friends, everything was fine. They spent time together and had fun. They did a lot together, but there were always underlying comments that were made by her friend that made her feel bad or inadequate. She said that in recent years, she could not disagree with her friend on anything without the consequences of a lecture and a long list of everything she said or did that was wrong. She said that she often ended up in tears because of the hurtful things her friend said. I asked why she stayed in the friendship. She responded that they had been friends too long to just end it. This leads us to the second common reason people stay in a place of devalue: loyalty.

Dr. James Kane is considered the leader in the science of loyalty. He states, "The brain seeks out three things: trust, belonging, and purpose. If you provide people with this, then they will be loyal to you." When it comes to staying loyal to someone who devalues you, the loyalty can be traced back to the beginning of the relationship. At the beginning of a job, a marriage, or a friendship, trust is built. A sense of belonging is fostered and this solidifies purpose. However, when devaluing begins, trust is eroded, but belonging and purpose are clung to. Let's use a job for an example. You start a new job; you get to know your co-workers, you build friendships, you problem-solve together, you have inside jokes, you see the pictures of each other's families on desks; you belong. What you are doing gives you purpose. There is no need to distrust. And then a shift happens. Maybe because of the friendship and team spirit that has been built, you are asked to do things for the sake of the team. Maybe it is picking up the slack for a co-worker, and that co-worker then gets a promotion because they have a more charismatic personality. Then when a new person is hired, you are expected to continue what you did before, picking up the slack. Maybe you try to talk to a supervisor about this but are dismissed, or they deflect by telling you the mistakes you have made. Maybe you find out the salary of someone who does the same job is more than the salary you make and you have been there longer. There could be numerous reasons for the trust to begin to break due to devaluing behaviors, but you stay because you have belonging, you have purpose.

This was the main issue for me in staying at a particular job where I was devalued. I have always been a loyal person. For a person who has been in a cycle of devalue for some time, seeking out trust, belonging, and purpose is important. However, when we lose trust due to devaluing tactics, but stay for the sense of belonging and purpose, we become double-minded. Being double-minded means you are wavering in your mind, vacillating in your thoughts and feelings. This can lead to insincerity and hypocrisy. Staying somewhere or staying in a relationship where you are devalued and trust has been broken, and then, using that same place to claim belonging and purpose will make you unstable in all your ways.

This is something that really resonates with me. When I was in my devaluing job, I was trying my best to stay and rise above because I felt like I belonged, but I had become unstable. I was emotional, easily offended, and self-righteous. More importantly, I began to feel justified in my double-mindedness. This is a dangerous place to be in because it takes you down a path of becoming a Devaluer to those who have devalued you. We never want to use our devaluing situation to become a Devaluer. That is where bitterness, resentment, and ideas of revenge sit and multiply within our spirit. It was at this time in my life that I heard God say, "Don't let loyalty become idolatry." I was stopped in my tracks. That was exactly what I had done. I had allowed loyalty to become idolatry. Remaining loyal had become the most important thing; more important than my health and well being, more important than the strain on my family, more important than the insomnia and anxiety, more important than the stress, more important than the voice of God; loyalty at any cost. An idolater is a person that admires intensely and often blindly. When you place loyalty over all else, the desire for belonging and purpose override the devaluing that is taking place. Clinging wholeheartedly to loyalty, blindly and intensely, keeps us in a place of devalue.

When I was in my devaluing relationship in high school, some important people in my life saw signs of what I was experiencing, and encouraged me to begin counseling with a pastor. I was asked in my first session to write down hurtful things that had been said to me. Here is what I wrote: "Your thoughts do not matter. Your concerns do not matter. You are stupid. You are worthless. You are ugly. You are untalented. You should not speak up for yourself. You will never have the courage to do what you want to do. You are not strong. You are not smart. Your voice means nothing. Your feelings are just dramatic. Your desire to be valued is prideful. You deserve how you are treated. You will always be lonely. You will always be sad. You will always be less than everyone else." The pastor read it and got tears in his eyes. He said, "This is a lot. You have been told so many lies. Now I want you to flip the paper over and write down all the people who have said these things and we are going to discuss each one." I flipped over the paper and wrote one name, "me". The pastor was expecting a long list of names. Those statements had not been made by my parents. They had not been made by my teachers. They had not been made by my friends. And though many of the ideas had been presented through the actions of my boyfriend, they had not been said by him. It was me. I had said those statements to myself, often and loudly and without remorse. A third reason we stay in a place of devalue is because we are the Devaluer.

This is a tough one. How do you separate yourself from the Devaluer if the Devaluer is you? We all have points in our lives where we devalue ourselves, but for most people, they can move on, pull themselves up, and find their value. Maybe they had a bad day or a bad week, but the end is in sight. For others, the devaluing cycle continues consistently and they become their own Devaluer. When you devalue yourself, you use the same tactics on yourself that other Devaluers use. You DISMISS your own thoughts and feelings by saying things like, "I shouldn't feel that way" or "I should just be quiet." You DEFLECT by reminding yourself of all the mistakes you have made. You DEMEAN yourself with a barrage of thoughts and accusations that could go toe to toe with the meanest and most powerful of Devaluers. Devaluing yourself can be more than words. You can neglect your health and stop all self-care. You can detach from people around you. You can ignore the signs and symptoms of depression. These are all ways that we devalue ourselves. If you desire to move from a cycle of devalue to a pattern of value, you have to acknowledge how you treat yourself. If you are in this place now, stick with me. We will soon discuss how you can begin healing and valuing yourself.

Buffering, loyalty, and self-devaluing are three of the most common reasons we stay in devaluing situations, however, there are many more reasons. A girl auditioned for a dance team and was turned down because of her body. For her, this was where her devalue began. She stayed in future devaluing situations because she felt she would not be accepted anywhere else. A teenaged boy was expelled from his school for one mistake. He was not even given the chance to speak for himself about the situation. For him, this is where his devalue began. He stayed in future devaluing situations because he felt silence was required of him. A young girl was violated by someone she loved. For her, this is where the devalue began. She stayed in future devaluing situations because she felt the known of a bad situation was better than the unknown. A woman's trust was broken when her boyfriend cheated on her. For her, this is where the devalue began. She stayed in future devaluing situation because always trusting someone was too painful. The list could go on and on. For every devalued person there is a reason they stay. If no one has told you that before, please hear it now. No reason is a good enough reason. You do not need to be a buffer. You do not need to remain loyal. You do not need to listen to your own words that tear you down. You will be accepted. You will have a voice. You can step into the unknown. You can trust again.

Chapter 4

Step 4 - Understanding the Deception of Devalue

Ever since I can remember, my mom has had a fancy jewelry box filled with earrings and rings. When I was little, it was like a box of treasures. I would try on rings and hold up earrings to see how they would look. Once, when I was young, I found a diamond ring. I was convinced it was my mother's engagement ring. It was a little cloudy, but so beautiful. I just knew it had to be real even though it was lying in the corner of the bottom drawer. In the closet, my mom kept a jar of a red solution that cleaned jewelry. I got the cleaner down and soaked the ring in it, knowing it would reveal something my mom had not seen; something that blocked her from seeing it for what it was. Otherwise, she would wear it always. Who would ever take off a real diamond ring? Once it was cleaned, I noticed a few nicks in the band, but it was still beautiful. I wore it on my thumb and noticed if I squeezed it on both sides, it fit better. I walked to my friend's house, moving my thumb back and forth, so the ring would sparkle in the sun. I had found a real diamond. It was so beautiful. When I got to my friend's house, I showed her the ring and told her it was my mom's engagement ring, and it was a real diamond. She was equally impressed with its glory. She told her mom to come see. When her mom heard, she was worried that I had brought my mom's expensive diamond engagement ring over. She looked at it with squinted eyes; head tilted to the side, and asked me if I was sure it was real. I assured her it was. She tied it on a string around my neck so I would not lose the beautiful ring. Wearing it around my neck, I felt some kind of way. It was now a ring and a necklace. I could look down and see it. I could feel it sway as I walked. I felt special. Without me knowing, my friend's mom called my mom and let her know that I had taken her engagement ring, but it was now safely secured on a string around my neck. When I got home, my mom told me that the ring was not her engagement ring. It was, in fact, not a real diamond. It was fake; something called cubic zirconia. It was inexpensive, and my mom was slightly embarrassed that I had said it was her engagement ring. I felt the glamour leave, the glitz fall from my shoulders. The special feeling of having something valuable and expensive was gone. It was fake. It was not real, but oh, did it look real! I had seen the cloudiness in the ring. I had seen the nicks in the band. I had found it in the corner of the bottom drawer. I had felt it bend. I had seen the doubt in the eyes of my friend's mother. However, I pushed forward, believing it was real. I had deceived myself into thinking it was valuable. This is a problem that arises with devalue. There is often a part of us that is deceived into thinking the devaluing is not really taking place. We see some signs. We see the looks in others' eyes, but we convince ourselves that it is not happening. This deception can be applied to the one being devalued or to the Devaluer.

No one wants to believe that someone is intentionally devaluing them, and I have come to believe that it is seldom the case. Most Devaluers have an arrogance and pride to them. They often think of themselves as put together. Strong. Confident. They may even think that they value themselves. We are not going to get into the mindset of a Devaluer in this book, however; just like there are many reasons for individuals to accept a life of devalue, there are many reasons why someone becomes a Devaluer. The important thing to note is that most Devaluers do not know they are Devaluers, and this is where deception comes into play. A boss, or spouse, or parent, or friend who devalues you, may, in fact, believe they are doing you a favor by shutting down your voice. They may think you do not have anything to add more important than what they have to add and you can learn from them. They may believe that shutting down your dreams is the kind thing to do because they do not see you reaching them. They may even start their devaluing sentences with, "You know I love you, but..." Value to them has a whole other meaning. Value for them begins with them. Their value, not yours, is of utmost importance.

When my first child was born, my husband and I were very conservative in how we raised him. We have since loosened up, much to the relief of our three subsequent children, and much to the dismay of our oldest. When it came time for Christmas, we did not want to tell our son that Santa was real. We told him the story of Saint Nicholas and explained that he was a nice man who did nice things but had lived a long time ago. We told him that the presents under the tree were from family and friends. This posed some issues during the Christmas holidays that we did not foresee. At Christmastime, when he was four, I took him to the store to get some wrapping paper and gifts tags. When we were in the check out, the cashier said, "Hi, Buddy. Are you excited for Santa to come in a few weeks?" My son looked at the cashier and said, "Santa is dead." I have yet to receive a dirtier look than was given to me by the cashier and the woman in line behind me. When our son started school, we would tell him that some of his friends believed Santa brought them gifts, and it was okay to let them play that game with their families, and he shouldn't tell them that Santa isn't bringing them gifts. However, our son is a black and white kind of thinker. He also likes to share knowledge that he has with those around him. His kindergarten teacher called me in early December to ask if I could speak to my son about "the whole Santa thing." She told me the class had been singing, "Santa Clause is Coming to Town," and it went something like this:

33

Class: You better watch out, you better not cry, you better not pout I'm telling you why. Santa Clause is coming to town.

My son: No, he isn't.

Class: He sees you when you're sleeping.

My son: No, he doesn't.

Class: He sees when you're awake.

My son: No, he doesn't.

Class: He knows if you've been bad or good, so be good for goodness sake.

My son: He can't come to town because he's dead.

She asked him to keep his comments to himself, but told me how the entire class jumped to Santa Clause's defense. They told my son that he was real, he was alive, he was coming to town, and he did have a list. My son had the truth, but it was not received well.

Though this is a funny story that has made us laugh over the years, the point is that when the truth of a situation is ready to be spoken, if the hearer has not been on a journey of self-discovery, the truth will not be received because the hardest type of deception to break is self-deception. When you apply this to Devaluers, you must understand that you will very rarely get a resolution to your devaluing situation by simply trying to tell the Devaluer that they are, in fact, a Devaluer. They have deceived themselves into thinking that they do the things they do for a good reason; and in all honesty, they most likely do not even think of you that much. They are too self-focused.

Though Devaluers can operate from a place of deception, devalued individuals can also be in a place of self-deception. Like my story of the sparkly "diamond" ring that showed many clear signs of not being real, we can ignore the signs of being devalued. One thing about those who are being devalued is that they quite often become people pleasers. The mindset is one of gaining value, even if this mindset is subconsciously by default. The thinking is, the more people pleased, the less likely the list of Devaluers will grow. However, this is where we can deceive ourselves by thinking that if we can just do what people ask, if we can just go above and beyond, if we can just fix problems we weren't even asked to fix, if we can just smile and go with the flow, we will be valuable. Value does not come from being perfect. Value does not come from fixing everyone's problems. Value does not come from taking on an overbearing workload. Value does not come from being a "yes" man or woman. Some common statements from those who are deceiving themselves into thinking they are not being devalued are: "he's just too busy to take the time to listen to me," "I'm just too needy," "her position is too important to care about my workload," "he's been through a lot so it's ok for him to act this way," "I'm fine," "I'll just do it;" and on and on the list goes. If you are going to move from a place of devalue to value, you have to accept and admit that you are being devalued. You cannot worry about why the Devaluer acts the way they do or try to justify their actions. Sometimes, this deception comes from assuming we have a relationship that is not really there.

When I was young, I lived next door to a family with three boys. My brothers and I would play with them in our backyards. We had a pool. They had a hammock. We would catch the toads that lived in the yard and make little houses for them out of sticks and leaves. One day, the way I felt around the youngest boy started to change, and my brother said I had a crush on him. I was not quite sure what it meant, so I asked one of my friends. She told me it meant that he and I were going to get married. She said that we, in fact, had to plan the wedding. We got to work. We decided the marriage would take place in about one week's time. My friend said she would be the person to marry us. We decided to invite our other friends to come. It would take place in the boy's backyard. We picked my outfit, a jean skirt, white shirt, and sandals. We decided we would make lemonade, and I would bring the chocolate pudding cups that we loved to eat for a snack. The only problem was that no one told the boy this was about to take place. He had no idea. On the day of the wedding, all our friends came to the backyard. There was so much giggling. When the boy came out, I told him we were getting married. He did what any boy at the age of ten would do. He ran. I, of course, chased him, and behind me was half the neighborhood. I remember that he was fast, really fast, and I couldn't catch him. My friend, who was going to marry us, suggested we tie him to the tree once he came back. By the time he returned, most of the crowd had gone home, the lemonade had been drunk, and the empty pudding cups laid on the ground. Though we did have some rope, we decided not to tie him to a tree. He saw me standing in his yard, ran past me, went inside, and locked his door. Things were slightly awkward after that. Needless to say, I thought we had a relationship we did not have.

Real relationships are hard to define in the culture that we live in. It used to be that a relationship could be defined by one on one conversations that resulted in connection. Conversations used to take time and effort; but now, in the tech age we live in, conversations go on all day and all night, without much effort. Texting, DM'ing, emailing, and posting on pages and timelines has taken the place of true conversation. We can text while we are doing five other things. We are not necessarily focused on and engaging with a person just because we are texting them. Texting someone an emoji can replace thinking of a true response to give. Liking someone's post can take the place of spending actual time getting to know them. We can have 600 friends or followers on social media and still have no true relationships. We can see snapshots of someone's life every single day, but never speak to them or engage with them when we see them in person. This has made relationships hard to define. What does it mean to have a relationship with someone?

There are many definitions of the word *relationship*. The one I like best is "the state of being connected," and the reason I like this definition is because of what "connected" means. *Connected* means "brought together or into contact so that a real or notional link is established." I like this because it says "real or notional." *Notional* means "existing only in theory or as a suggestion or idea." This means that a relationship can be real or notional. Like my relationship with my neighbor when I was ten, it was a notion, an idea that only existed in theory. Basically, it boils down to this. You can have a notional relationship that is one-sided, an idea, a theory, or you can have a real relationship that is two-sided. Within real relationships, you can have a healthy or an unhealthy relationship.

If you were to do an internet search for the characteristics of a healthy relationship, you would receive somewhere around 600 million results. Among those results, you would find characteristics like passion, common interests, compromise, problem-solving, understanding, individuality, self-love, and shared sense of humor. However, there are four characteristics that experts agree on over and over again. A healthy relationship has respect, trust, honesty, and good communication. These characteristics can easily be one-sided. Sometimes, if we have respect for someone, we trust them, are honest with them, and communicate our thoughts and feelings; we can assume that they are doing the same. This is not always the case. The relationship between the Devaluer and the Devalued is not a healthy relationship. The Devalued individual can stay stuck in deception by assuming a relationship that is not there. It may be hard to accept, but being in a family with someone, being married to someone, working with someone, following someone on social media, or dating someone does not equal having a healthy relationship with them.

I used to work as a server at a hotel restaurant when I was first married and my husband and I were finishing college. I had a co-worker that was funny and outgoing. She brought me out of my shell. She would always come to work with hilarious stories, and she would have the most interesting things happen at her tables. We worked together for a while and would talk through our entire shift. If it were slow, we would wander through the hotel together. Our favorite thing to do was to go to the lobby and see who was checking in. We would assign a story to their lives based on what they brought in and how they interacted with the check-in clerks. My friend would say things like, "Oh, here comes Linda. She has three cats and a limo driver at home. She is not sure how to check in without her assistant, but he is parking the car." As our conversations continued, we would share things about our lives and even discussed any problems we faced. I would even give her some of my tables when I knew her rent was late in order to help her out. We were working together on New Year's Eve, and it was busy. We had to wait on our tables and help do extra tasks in the kitchen as well. After serving a table, I looked down at my hand and realized that I had cut my finger slicing lemons and was bleeding, but I had already served water to my table. I went to my friend and asked her what to do because I had broken a rule by cutting lemons without wearing a specialized glove. I was afraid of the manager's response and worried if blood was on the glasses I had brought to the table. My friend told me to get a Band-Aid and then go to my table with new waters and to tell them that I thought they needed water with more ice and then exchange the glasses. She said that way the situation was taken care of and the manager would not need to find out. I went to get a Band-Aid and when I came out the manager was waiting for me. He said that my friend informed him that I had cut lemons without the glove and had cut myself then served my table getting blood on a glass. He said he had sent her to take care of that table, and in fact, had given her all my other tables because I now had to clean the lemon slicer and all the other equipment around it. He told me that I had broken two rules; cutting lemons and not reporting an injury. I tried to explain, but he did not want to hear it. I started to clean the equipment when my friend came into the kitchen to pick up food. We made eye contact, and before I could say anything, she said, "What? I'm not your friend. Haven't you been a server before? It's all about getting the most tables and the best tables. I saw an opportunity and I took it." I was shocked and hurt. I thought that we had a relationship. I RESPECTED how hard she worked. I TRUSTED her with my problems. I was HONEST when she asked for advice. We COMMUNICATED every day that we worked together. So how do we interpret what my co-worker and I had? First of all, we did have a real relationship. We were connected. However, it was an unhealthy relationship because one person was genuine, and the other was using the relationship for their gain.

In all relationships, we are on a trajectory moving towards each other. As we get to know someone and they get to know us, we move closer together. Every relationship has a moment where we decide if we want to keep moving forward, stay where we are, or go in another direction. Each individual in a relationship can make a different decision, and this is based on perception. I was recently with a couple who has been dating for over two years. She jokingly said to her boyfriend, "On the count of three, let's say what percentage it is that we will most likely get married." After the count of three, she said 80% and he said 50%. They are two people in a relationship, moving on a trajectory towards each other, but with different perceptions of where the relationship is in its current state. We can feel the relationship is in one place, and the other person can see it in a completely different place. We have to look for those moments, moments where the other person may back away a little, or not answer a question directly, or start texting less after we share a particularly heavy problem with them. Or moments where they draw closer to us, ask deeper questions, or offer support in a difficult time. These moments help us gauge where each person is in a relationship. Where devalued individuals get stuck in self-deception is when they gauge a relationship as deeper than it is, without picking up on these moments. If I had been more in tune to my relationship with my co-worker, I would have noticed how she lamented not having rent money, asking for my tables, but then came in the next day with an expensive new tattoo. I maybe would have asked myself if she was using me to get tables. I would have noticed that she knew the details of my life, my husband's name, where I went to college, and where I grew up, yet I knew few details about her life. She always spoke in generalities. To step out of a place of deception, we have to really evaluate the relationships we are in. We cannot stay in a place of devalue because we assume a relationship is something that it is not.

Chapter 5

Step 5 - Understanding the Process of Stepping out of Devalue

Process is a series of actions or steps taken in order to achieve a particular end. It is important. It is found everywhere. I have been a teacher for many years, and the number one thing I have to do every year, the first week of school, is to set up all the processes in the classroom. If I do not do this, I will have chaos. How do you turn your homework in? What do you do if you need to use the restroom? What if you have a question? I have taught kindergarten, all the way to seniors in high school, and it does not change. The process is of utmost importance. The same is true of teachers. Teachers need to be told the process that the administration would like them to follow. How do I ask for a day off? How do I send a student to the office? What do I do to set up a field trip? Without process, there is chaos. I am a science teacher, and one of my favorite subjects to teach is genetics. One year I taught an honors genetics class for juniors and seniors. We spent a semester breeding Drosophila melanogaster, the basic fruit fly. There was a very specific process we needed to follow for our experimentation. We were breeding the flies to see how many offspring had white eyes and how many had red eyes. In order to check on our fruit flies, we needed to put them to sleep with a special solution, so we could inspect them closely. Our flies lived in tubs with breathable lids. The process was as follows: Step 1, dip the cotton swab in the solution; Step 2, take the lid and move it slightly to the side while sliding in the cotton swab; Step 3, once the flies fall asleep, remove the cotton swab; Step 4, remove the lid; Step 5, transfer the flies to a tray; Step 6, use a magnifying glass to inspect and take notes; a simple 6-step process. The first day that we went through the process as a class, I got to Step 2 and said, "take the lid…" and as students sometimes do, some did not let me complete my sentence and they assumed I was going to say "take the lid off." They removed the lid, releasing the fruit flies into the classroom, which soon went into the halls, which soon went into the school. We had a slight infestation due to one missed step in a process. Students could be seen in the halls swatting away our pesky little escapees for weeks. Process is important. When moving from a place of devalue to value, there is a process. Following the process offers the best results.

How exactly does someone move from devalue to value? We have covered what devalue is, how Devaluers act, reasons we stay in a place of devalue, and the self-deception that we can remain in. By now, you should be able to recognize whether or not you are in a specific devaluing situation or have been in the past. If you are unsure, go back to the questions listed in chapter one. Ask yourself each question and answer honestly. If you have someone in your life that is trustworthy and gives you wise advice, listen to what they may be saying to you about your situation. Those who see a relationship from the outside can see things that those in the relationship may be blinded from seeing. Situations vary from person to person. Your devaluing situation may look different from someone else's situation. It could be a marriage, a dating relationship, a friendship, a family relationship, a job, or a church ministry. I have shared many examples of situations where I was devalued, from dating relationships to family situations to jobs. You may be in multiple devaluing situations. You may have left your devaluing situation, but still carry the hurts and scars from it. Whatever the case may be, you can move to a place of value. The first step is to acknowledge the devaluing situation. I will say it again, acknowledge your situation. Say, "I am being devalued" or "I have been devalued." It may be uncomfortable, but say it aloud. Say it to yourself in the mirror. There is power in acknowledgement. There is the power of life and death in the tongue. Bringing something out into the open, releasing it from a hidden place, and accepting that it is true is the first step to empowering yourself to move forward. After you acknowledge your devaluing place, choose a positive statement that you will repeat to yourself through the process. My statement was spoken to me by a spiritual leader in my life, and I took it on wholeheartedly. My statement is, "I am powerful and I am valuable." This is the next step in moving forward; you have acknowledged where you are and where you have been, now it is time to acknowledge where you are going. I did not feel powerful or valuable when I first made the statement. I felt defeated, worried, powerless, and really just scared. I was scared that what I was stepping out of was the only place I deserved to be. I was afraid that there was not a future for me. However, I said it anyways, "I am powerful. I am valuable." I said it multiple times a day. I said it to myself. I wrote it in a journal. When I was alone in the car, I would test saying it aloud to see what it sounded like. Choose your statement and say it often. If you are in a place where you cannot create a statement, borrow mine. You are powerful. You are valuable.

Once you have acknowledged the areas of devalue in your life and decided on a statement to move forward, you need to make a plan. You need to be ready to confront or remove yourself from your devaluing situation. Whether you confront the situation or remove yourself from it is determined by the situation itself. When I found myself in a particular devaluing situation, I made an abrupt decision to leave. To remove myself from the situation. I was broken-hearted because there were things I loved that I was leaving behind. I had not yet acknowledged my devalue and did not even know that the concept existed. I just knew that it wasn't right. I knew that something needed to change. I cried for days and tried to move forward, but I was stuck. I eventually went back to the same situation because I did not yet understand that I was not valued there. I still believed that I could fix the situation. I believed that if I just did enough, I would be valued. It wasn't until several months later that I stepped away with a completely different mindset. In my situation, I decided to remove myself instead of confronting the devalue. I felt that after all I had experienced, confronting the situation would not have a positive result. This was a situation that I could remove myself from and move forward without damaging other positive relationships.

Removing yourself is not always the answer. Sometimes the devalue needs to be confronted. However, you have to remember the tactics of Devaluers. Simply confronting the situation on your own, without a plan, can yield negative instead of positive results. I am a big proponent of professional assistance in situations that involve a marriage or family relationship. It is important to plan what you want to confront. Write it out. Have examples. Decide where you are willing to compromise and where you are not. Involve a professional counselor, pastor, or mentor. It may be uncomfortable to have to confront devalue in the presence of someone else, but if your end goal is restoration and rebuilding, you will need assistance. If the other person in the relationship refuses to participate, then go yourself, and work out your plan with a professional. Even if you feel like ending the relationship or situation is what needs to happen, I suggest speaking to a professional first. If involving a professional, pastor, or mentor is not an option, remember, you have the power. You are in control. If you need to confront through a phone call so there is physical space between you and the other person, you can do that. If you need to write a letter to the person, do that. Remember, you are valuable, and as a valued human spirit, there is no need for you to confront with sarcasm, meanness, yelling, or name-calling. A simple explanation while remaining calm is the best approach. You can also walk away if you need to. You are powerful. You can move forward.

What if you have already left your devaluing relationship or situation, and yet you harbor hurts, scars, or even bitterness, what can you do? Follow the same procedure. Acknowledge that you were in a place of devalue. Create a statement about yourself and declare it. I have been in this place and I replayed so many conversations over and over in my head. This is what we tend to do when we are hurt. We nurse the hurts to remind us of the wrong done to us. Dwelling on those hurts will take us to a place of bitterness. Bitterness can have negative effects on our emotions and our physical bodies. Studies show that holding onto bitterness can affect metabolism, organ function, and immunity. It allows the devalue to continue to have a hold on us. You also need to write down what you would say if you were confronting your situation. Get all your thoughts and feelings out. This will help you to stop replaying the situations over again in your head. Then, make a list of all that you learned by coming out of your devaluing relationship. Write your lessons in a positive light. Instead of saying, "I learned not to trust anyone," say, "I learned to be cautious when placing my trust in someone." Take the very way in which you were devalued and speak to it in a positive light. If your devalue made you feel inadequate, write the statement, "I am more than enough." If your devalue made you feel unloved, write the statement, "I am loved." You want to take the positive from what you have learned. Finally, write a thank you note; yes, a thank you note. You won't be sending this note. It is for you. Use your devaluing moments as a thank you. Here is the thank you note I wrote to the Devaluers in my life:

"Dear Devaluers,

Thank you. Thank you for showing me that I am worth so much more. Thank you for helping me learn to speak up for myself and to know that seeing the value in another person should be intrinsic. I learned that my value should naturally and unquestionably speak to the value in others. Thank you for helping me learn, though it was a hard lesson, that no amount of work I do or love I give can force another person to value me. Because of you, I value those who value me so much more. They received the parts and pieces of me that were broken and put them back together, because even in a broken state, they saw my value. I now have a freedom I did not have when I was with you. I have the freedom to value myself."

We have spent enough time talking about devalue. Let's move forward and learn more about value, where it comes from, and how to live in a place of value from this point forward.

Chapter 6

Step 6 - Understanding Value Comes from God

Imagine, if you will, being a woman born into the "wrong" family according to cultural standards. Your only prospect is to become a slave. Once enslaved, you, your being, your body, your future, your present, all belong to those who have purchased you. You must do as they ask. You must do as they see fit. This was the life of Hagar in the Book of Genesis. She was the Egyptian slave of Sarah and Abraham. Many studies suggest even her birth name was taken from her, as *Hagar* is interpreted to mean "the stranger" or "the alien," and sounds similar to a Hebrew phrase used for "other." She was called, not by a name, but rather, a generic label. She was forced to marry Abraham and conceive a child. While Hagar was pregnant, Sarah complained to Abraham, who was husband to both Sarah and Hagar. Sarah complained, in essence, about Hagar's attitude. Abraham told Sarah to do what she liked with Hagar. We do not know exactly what it entailed, but Genesis

16 tells us that Sarah "mistreated" Hagar. The word *mistreated* in Hebrew means, "to deal harshly with, to oppress, to punish or inflict pain upon." Sarah was most likely beating Hagar, and Hagar ran for her life. She found herself in the desert near a spring when the angel of the Lord appeared to her and told her to return to Sarah, but not before he speaks a blessing over Hagar, giving her the same blessing he had given to Sarah and Abraham. He tells Hagar that He will increase her descendants until they are too numerous to count, taking the sacred promise made to Sarah and Abraham, and extending it to Hagar. The angel of the Lord then tells her that she will give birth to a son and will name him Ishmael. Hagar may have been caught up in the middle of Sarah's disobedience to God, but God saw and He knew. Here is where things get interesting. Hagar, an Egyptian, not a Hebrew, not raised in Hebrew culture, not aware of the God of the Hebrews, nor who He was, gives Him a name. She gives him the name *El Roi*, which means "you are the God who sees me." Naming God was not the job of the people. It was almost blasphemy. But Hagar was not concerned with what the proper thing to do was in terms of speaking to God or using His name properly or following a religious tradition. She took what she experienced and she expressed it to God. God, in turn, did the same thing. He named her son Ishmael, which means "God hears." Hagar acknowledged that God saw her, and God acknowledged that He also heard her. He had come to her in her time of need and taken what was broken and turned it into a blessing. He took

her devalue at the hands of Sarah and reminded Hagar of her value. Hagar's value was not assigned that day. Hagar's value, as all of ours, was assigned before she was born.

For some individuals, their feeling of devalue comes from the circumstances of their conception and birth. Individuals who were conceived by "accident" or by force or from other negative experiences at times feel that their life started in a place of devalue. An absent mother, an absent father, adoption, and many other circumstances can give someone the feeling that they were not valued from the beginning. No matter the origin of your entrance into this world, you were meant to be. You were designed by God. You were destined by Him. You are absolutely, unashamedly, unconditionally, irrevocably, valuable to Him. He values you. Don't just take my word for it. I will prove it to you.

Psalm 139 says before He formed you He knew you. It says He made all the delicate inner parts of your body while in your mother's womb. One singular cell in a developing baby all of a sudden begins to beat, and is instantly joined by more cells that somehow remarkably beat at the same exact rhythm, the beginning of the human heart. This is God using His creative power, the creative power that made you. Psalm 139 also says that God's thoughts about you are vast and if you were to try and count them, they would outnumber the grains of sand. Scientists estimate that at any given time there are seven quintillion, five hundred quadrillion grains of sand on the earth, yet God's thoughts about you outnumber the grains of sand. He values you. And if you think that is an unfathomable number of grains of sand, let's talk about the stars. Isaiah 40 tells us, "Lift up your eyes and look to the heavens; who created all these? He who brings out the stars one by one and calls fourth each of them by name because of his great power and mighty strength, not one of them missing." Yes, the number of grains of sand on earth is over seven quintillion, but the estimated number of stars in the heavens is seventy sextillion, which is 70 followed by 21 zeros multiplied by 70 followed by 21 zeros multiplied by 70 followed by 21 zeros, and God calls each one by name. That is great power and mighty strength, yet Luke tells us that what God really cares about are the very hairs on your head, which He has numbered, and that is more important to Him than the grains of sand on the shore or stars in the sky or sparrows that fly or lilies in the field. He values you.

One of the quintessential pictures of a mother and child is one of a mother rocking her baby and singing a lullaby. It shows the bond of love between mother and child. Did you know that God Himself sings over you? Zephaniah 3 says, "For the Lord your God is living among you. He is a mighty savior. He will take delight in you with gladness. With his love, he will calm all your fears. He will rejoice over you with joyful songs." The word *rejoice* in Hebrew means "to spin around under the influence of a violent emotion, to dance." A word for word translation from the Hebrew reads like this: "Yahuwah your God in your midst, the Mighty One, will save; He will rejoice over you with gladness, He will quiet you with His love, He will dance over you with singing." The God who created quintillion grains of sand and all the stars in the universe sings and dances over you. He values you.

1 John 3 says, "See how great a love the Father has lavished on us that we should be called children of God!" Another version calls it the extravagant love of God. *Extravagant* means "spending much more than is necessary, excessively high: exceeding the bounds of reason, going beyond what is deserved or justifiable: wild, not within ordinary limits of probability, or other usual bounds." This is God's love for you that He demonstrated through Jesus. When you think about Jesus' death on the Cross and the grace it brought us, it fits the definition of extravagant. He spent so much, exceeding the bounds of human reason. He went beyond what was deserved or was justifiable because of His love. He did this for you because He values you. God's opinion of you is what matters. Understanding the way He values you is foundational to stepping into a place of value and breaking the cycle of devalue. No matter what you do or do not do, He values you. There is nothing you can do to make Him love you more and nothing you can do to make Him love you less. His value of you is what matters. His grace is what matters. Who you are in Jesus is what matters. Jesus is proud of you. He is rejoicing over you with singing because before you were born, He saw the moment you would read this and every day that came before and will come after. He goes before you. He values you.

God created you as a valuable treasure. His love for you and commitment to you are examples of just how valuable you are. However, we live in a fallen world that will tear us to pieces. We are surrounded by individuals and systems that are sinful. We, ourselves, are slaves to sin without the redemptive power of Jesus. We were created to be valued, but the world, including ourselves, invites devalue in. Whatever God created as good, the enemy will use its counterpart for evil. Jesus came to seek and to save what was lost. He regularly and intentionally spoke to the devalued. He spoke life into them. He reminded them of their value.

In John 4, we read the story of the Samaritan woman at the well. Jesus and His disciples traveled to Samaria, but this was not customary. It was customary for Jews to avoid Samaritans. It was customary for men to avoid women. However, Jesus had other plans. He was at the well, waiting on His disciples to bring food. The Samaritan woman came to draw water, and Jesus asked her for a drink. She was surprised because He was a male Jew speaking to her, a Samaritan woman. Jesus told her that He could give her living water, and then He called her out. He asked about her husband, and when she said that she did not have one, He replied by saying, "You are right when you say you have no husband. The fact is, you have had five husbands, and the man you now have is not your husband." The woman at the well was devalued by the men in her life. She was devalued by the community she lived in because of her shameful lifestyle. She undoubtedly devalued herself. Jesus spoke life to her. He challenged her to the living water only he can offer, and when she accepted, she told the whole village, and many came to know Jesus as their messiah. He went out of His way to travel through Samaria, knowing He would encounter her, just so He could show her how valuable she was.

In the book of John, Jesus is teaching in the temple and the self-righteous Pharisees bring Him a woman caught in the act of adultery. Only the woman was brought. The man is never mentioned. The Pharisees humiliate her, threaten her, ask for her death, and devalue her. They use her as a pawn to try and trick Jesus into breaking the law. Jesus agrees to her stoning death, only if a Pharisee who has never sinned throws the first stone. Slowly, the maddening, death-hungry crowd leaves, and Jesus is left alone with the woman. I can picture this moment because I have had many of them with Jesus. Just me and Him. When I have messed up, when I feel broken, when I am lonely, when I beat myself up; He lovingly asks where my condemners are, and then reassures me that He does not condemn me. This is what He asked the woman, "Where are your accusers. Didn't even one of them condemn you?" Then He says, "Neither do I. Go and sin no more." He valued her with His words and His actions.

Jesus values the Devaluers as well. Zacchaeus was a tax collector. We read about him in Luke 19. Tax collectors were known to cheat people out of their money and use it to build their own wealth. We know that Zacchaeus was doing this. We know it because he admits it. He says that he will pay back all those he has cheated. Jesus finds Zacchaeus and invites Himself over for dinner. Imagine, a teacher, a rabbi, eating at the home of a sinner. All who saw Jesus do this were calling Jesus a guest of sinners. They meant it as a shameful label, but I think Jesus saw it as a compliment. Zacchaeus was a Devaluer. He literally cheated the poor, placing more value on himself than them, yet Jesus came to him and loved him.

When Jesus encountered John the Baptist, John felt unworthy, not valuable enough to be in the presence of Jesus or even untie Jesus' shoes, but Jesus valued John and gave him a place of honor by allowing John to baptize Him. When Jesus encountered Peter, He saw his lack of fish and the economic toil it would have. He provided fish for Peter in such abundance that multiple ships had to come and help with the load. Peter fell at Jesus' feet, filled with awareness of his own sin; he could not be in Jesus' presence. But Jesus valued Peter and called him to become a fisher of men. The widow at Nain was bearing the loss of her only son, her loss of protection, her loss of being provided for. When Jesus saw her, "his heart went out to her" and He valued her. He valued her in that moment, and He valued her future. He knew what her future would be if she were left without a husband or a son, and He had compassion. He said simple words, "Don't cry," and raised her son from the dead.

Wherever you may be in your pursuit of Jesus, know that He assigned value to you before you were even formed in your mother's womb. He loves you and calls you by name. Ultimately, to move from a place of devalue to value, we have to accept that we were created with value by a loving Father. When we understand our value through God's eyes, it opens the door for us to value ourselves.

Chapter 7

Step 7 - Understanding How to Value Yourself and Others

When my daughter was four years old, we went to a fall festival for Halloween at a local church. Being Mexican-American, my daughter had the perfect olive skin and long dark hair to dress up as Jasmine from Aladdin. In her costume, she really did look like the character. We even added a little lamp for her to carry. There were many activities at the event, and it was to culminate with a costume award ceremony at the end. We were told that judges would be walking around and looking at costumes during the event. When the time came for the ceremony, my daughter looked at me and said, "Mommy, I just know I'm gonna win. I look just like Jasmine." I gave her an obligatory mom speech about how nice her costume was, but reminded her that if she did not win, we would be happy for the girl who did. As the ceremony began, they showed the prize for the boy who would win, racetracks with Matchbox cars; and for the girl who won, a princess jewelry set. My daughter looked at me and said, "That will look perfect on me." My husband and I exchanged glances. They announced the boy who won, complete with a drum roll and applause from the crowd. The emcee then said, "And the winner in the girl's category for best costume goes to, drum roll please," and as the drum began to roll, my daughter got up with all the confidence in the world and started down the aisle. My husband tried to grab her, but she was too quick. She sashayed down the aisle, looking to her left and her right, smiling from ear to ear. The emcee looked at the drummer, then to the crowd. My daughter arrived at the front just as the drum roll stopped. No, her name had not been announced. No, she had not seen the results. She just valued herself so much she had no doubt in her mind the prize was hers. The emcee finished by saying, "How did you know? The winner is Jasmine." My daughter claimed her prize and returned to her seat, full of joy and pride. To this day, we do not know if she was the intended winner or if the emcee followed her lead. Children value themselves. They are concerned about their needs, their toys, their food, their space, and their agendas. We, as parents, cater to those needs, all while trying to instill in them a care for others. Self-value is normal, inherent even. However, somewhere along the way, we can lose the importance of valuing ourselves. Valuing yourself is one of the hardest steps to take. We have lots of names in our society for this: self-love, self-care, self-esteem, self-respect. But for some, it comes with ideas of selfishness, pride, or a lack of care for others. There are two main reasons we do not value ourselves.

The first reason we do not value ourselves is because we have been in a devaluing situation so long, we have adapted to what that situation requires of us. It may require keeping quiet, not sharing our thoughts, making sure everyone else is taken care of before we take care of ourselves; blending in. When we are in a place of devalue, we minimize ourselves to avoid drawing others' attention to the devalue, or to avoid drawing the Devaluer's attention. I did this often in a particular devaluing work environment. Sometimes my co-workers would point out a situation where they saw I was being devalued, and I would respond with, "Oh, it's okay, I love my job," or "I know how it came across, but that isn't what he meant," or "I prefer to work behind the scenes." Anything, really, to keep the attention off the fact that others were noticing. When we are in this state of mind, we learn to ignore our needs. When we are in this state of mind, proving our value is the most important thing. We are willing to work more hours, not asking off even to go to the doctor because we want to be seen as valuable. We are willing to do all the work in a relationship to the point of ignoring our need to spend time with friends, hoping we will finally be seen as a valuable person in the relationship. We ease all of the family drama; ignoring the stress that is building inside of us all in hopes that value will be assigned. When we step out of a devaluing situation, it feels uncomfortable and strange and off-balance and not normal to care for ourselves.

Another reason we devalue ourselves is because we have been taught, either outright or subtly, that self-value is wrong. How can this be? If you were raised in an altruistic or a Christian home, you may have been taught to put others before yourselves, taught to hate pride and love humility, taught to serve others, taught to meet the needs of people around you. This is actually a biblical principle. Philippians 2:3 says, "Do nothing from selfishness or empty conceit, but with humility of mind regard one another as more important than yourselves." This is a verse that is often used to convince or manipulate Christians into thinking that meeting their own needs and valuing themselves is not important or correct. However, we need to look at the verse in context. Philippians chapter two starts with the word "therefore." Whenever we see that word, we need to look before it to see what the "therefore" is referring to. In Philippians chapter one, Paul is showing his appreciation to the Church of Philippi, and encouraging them to live their faith together. At the end of chapter one, he encourages them to "stand firm in one spirit, with one mind, striving together." This speaks of a give and a take; living in unity, caring for other's needs, while they care for your needs. This leads into chapter two, where Paul continues speaking about encouragement, love, fellowship, affection, compassion, like-mindedness, unity, and intent of purpose. When we get to verse three, Paul has set the stage to show that he is speaking about how believers are to interact with one another. And in verse four, he goes on to say, "Do not *merely* look out for your own personal interests, but also for the interests of others." *Merely* means "only." He is instructing believers to be of the same mind, and to not only look out for their own interests, but also the interests of others. This does not mean overcommitting to events, ministries, or needs in the church. This does not mean doing for others while they do for no one. This does not mean that you are filled with pride if you look out for your needs. This does not mean it is a sin to say no. Jesus Himself needed time to Himself while ministering. He often slipped away from the crowds. Furthermore, Psalms tells us that God grants rest to those He loves. First Peter 2 tells us that when we accept Jesus into our lives, we become chosen, a priesthood, a nation, a people belonging to God "that we may proclaim the excellencies of him who called us out of darkness into his marvelous light." Can we proclaim His excellencies when we are worn down, overworked, unhealthy, or neglectful of our family? We cannot. If you have been taught that self-care is selfish or not a Christ-like principle, I am here to tell you that God intended for you to take care of yourself. You are the temple of the Holy Spirit. We are instructed in 1 Corinthians 6 to glorify God with our bodies. We cannot do that if we do not value ourselves.

I have recently been on a health journey. When I came out of my last devaluing situation, I found myself overworked, overweight, unhealthy, and stressed. I wasn't sleeping. I wasn't caring for my body or my spirit. The two go hand in hand. As we care for our spirit, we are prompted to care for our bodies because our spirit dwells within our body. I started with the basics that you have probably heard your whole life: drinking more water, going on walks, cooking healthy meals. These steps started me on a path of caring for myself. God intended for us to value and care for ourselves. Proverbs tells us, "Whoever gets sense loves his own soul." Ephesians tells us, "No one ever hated his own flesh, but nourishes and cherishes it, just as Christ does the church." Value yourself.

Sometimes it takes the voice of another to push us into valuing ourselves. Remember the story I told in chapter two about my college boyfriend belittling me in the lobby of his dorm? In that story, I spoke of an armchair stranger that told me I deserved better and asked the crucial question, "What are you doing with him?" That question made me begin to evaluate what exactly I *was* doing with him. I broke up with that boyfriend a few weeks later in January of 1995, and became intrigued by who the armchair stranger was. I began to notice him more around campus and especially noticed that as part of his job on the maintenance crew, he would wax the floor in front of the student office on the days I had office hours. He swears to this day it was a coincidence that he was waxing the floor on the day I happened to be in the office. I swear to this day it was not a coincidence at all. He ended up asking me out in February, we got engaged in March, and married in August. He did not know me or have any intention of dating me when he saw how I was being treated. I did not know him or have any intention of dating him when I responded to his statement by breaking up with my boyfriend. I can almost see how God was watching; smiling at the fact that we had no intentions, but He was causing our paths to cross in a way that would solidify in my heart before we even knew each other's name, that this man cared for my heart and the condition it was in. God is really awesome like that. My husband has valued me everyday since the beginning of our relationship. God used him to speak life to me and my brokenness. My husband has always encouraged me to value myself, and has helped me to see the times I am not treating myself in a valuable way. If you are having trouble valuing yourself, start looking and listening. Ask God to show you. Maybe it will be through a verse that you read, or the words of a friend or family member, or even the words of a stranger. At times, we need a push in the right direction. If you have not had that push, let reading this be the push that you need. You are precious to God. You are His. In Isaiah, God says, "Fear not, for I have redeemed you; I have summoned you by name; you are mine. When you pass through the waters, I will be with you; and when you pass through the rivers, they will not sweep over you. When you walk through the fire, you will not be burned; the flames will not set you ablaze." You have come through so much, and God has been with you. Do not fear, step forward into a place of value. You cannot fully move from a place of devalue until you value your spirit, soul, and body. Do this, so when it is time to "love your neighbor as yourself," you have a healthy understanding, in word and in practice, of what it means to love yourself.

As mentioned before, it is intrinsic to value others. In 2012, researchers were able to show that there is a specific part of the brain, the anterior insular cortex, that processes human empathy; a specific part of the brain created by God to allow us to offer empathy to others. There is also a part of the brain, the right supramarginal gyrus, that recognizes a lack of empathy and then makes necessary corrections to become empathetic. Studies also show that twins start purposefully interacting with one another in the womb as early as fourteen weeks gestation and that these interactions are not accidental but intentional. God created us to be intrinsically empathetic to each other, to interact intentionally with each other. We were created to fellowship and grow with one another. We were created to see the value in others, and when necessary, to help them see it in themselves.

When I went to Africa as an intern during college, I brought a lot of crafts and activities with me to do with the children. I knew that we spoke different languages and thought this would be a way to bridge the gap. I brought pieces of leather and different color beads with me. When I got them out, to my surprise, the adults wanted to learn how to do the craft as well. I showed them how to tie a knot in the middle of the leather pieces, add the beads, and tie a second knot. Finally, I showed them how to add the fastener and clasp it around their wrist. When we were done, a woman approached me with an interpreter and told me that she was there from another village and had never seen anything like what we made. She asked if I had extra. I had enough for about 100 more bracelets and gave her all that I had. The next day, the interpreter came and got me, and said he wanted to show me something. We went to the village that the woman was from. When we arrived, I saw that she had set up under a tree, and there was a line of people waiting. One by one, she called each person forward, showed them how to make the bracelet, fastened it on them, and then gave them the materials to make another. When I asked what she was doing, the interpreter said, "When we learn something new, a trade, a method, or a lesson, it becomes our responsibility to teach it to someone else." I was blown away. I will never forget the scene. She was passing on what she learned and giving each person the materials to pass it on to someone else. When you come out of a place of hurt or devalue, when you have overcome an obstacle, when you have survived an ordeal, peace and purpose can come from teaching others how to overcome.

One of the greatest joys I have had since coming out of a place of devalue is to be able to speak into the lives of others who are in the process of coming out of devalue themselves. We can, of course, accept love and sympathy from those in our lives who love us, but there is something powerful and life-affirming when someone who has been where you are says, "I understand." We have to remember some ground rules when we are speaking to someone who is in a place of devalue.

Remember chapter 5; there is a process to stepping out of devalue, and just because we can see it, and we know the freedom that comes after, does not mean others are ready to start their journey. Even while writing this book, I had to contact a friend and apologize. She and I were in a devaluing situation together, and she chose to get out. She was ready to go on the journey and begin the process. She tried to encourage me to do the same. Once she left the situation, I did not continue my friendship with her because it was hard for me, on some level, to see her freedom, when I did not yet understand what devalue even looked like.

One of the best ways to value others is to speak life to them, encourage them, ask questions about their life and their interests, their family and their pets. Let them know what you see in them. I had a friend speak to me during a difficult time where I was struggling with fear. She prayed over me that I would have the bravery of 1,000 armies. That is speaking life; when you see in someone something they do not see in themselves, and you speak it to them. Speaking life becomes second nature when you practice. It is as simple as telling a stranger that you love her nails or the fast food cashier that she has an amazing smile. It is telling the mom in line behind whose cart is filled with kids, that she is doing a good job. It is tipping a little extra at a restaurant and asking for the manager on the way out so you can say what excellent service you had. It is going up to your pastor after the sermon and mentioning something that really spoke to you. It is asking the other dog mom at the dog park questions about her dog while complimenting her. Every day, there are moments where you can speak kindly to someone and call out their value. It may be all they need. Speaking life and assigning value can also mean speaking the truth in love to someone you have a healthy relationship with. It may sound like, "You are so gifted and deserve to be treated with respect at your job." or "You are a loving and caring girlfriend. You deserve a boyfriend who sees and values those characteristics in you." This is better than saying, "Why do you put up with disrespect at your job?" or "Your boyfriend doesn't deserve you." For people who are in a situation that they have not yet acknowledged, speaking life brings more realization then speaking the truth in a negative manner. It is important to remember that we can value ourselves and value others at the same time. Being in a place of devalue teaches us to ignore ourselves and to excessively meet the needs of others in an attempt to be valued, but when we step out of a cycle of devalue and begin a pattern of value, we learn how to value ourselves as we value others.

Chapter 8

Conclusion

I am praying that you now have the tools you need to move forward. Here are the tools you should have in your toolbox. Tool number one: the ability to recognize devalue; if you need to, go back to chapter one and ask yourself the questions listed there again, and come back to it later as needed. The ability to recognize devalue is the first step towards freedom from devaluing situations. Tool number two: the ability to recognize the tactics of Devaluers; though Devaluers are different, their tactics are the same. Remember to look for signs of deflection, being dismissed, and demeaning behavior. There are questions in chapter two that you can ask yourself to gauge if you have a Devaluer in your life. Tool number three: the ability to recognize what keeps you from stepping out of a devaluing situation; you do not need to be a buffer, you do not need to let loyalty become idolatry, and you do not need to listen to your own words that bring you down. Determine in your mind that you will not make excuses. You will rise above and honor yourself. Tool number four: the ability to recognize deception, especially self-deception, and to speak the truth to your own soul; get serious with yourself. Get alone and analyze the situations in your life that are giving you pause, that are making you uneasy. God will reveal the truth to you. Tool number five: the ability to transition to a place of value; remember, it is a process. Make a plan. Decide how you want to proceed. You are in control. Get professional help if needed. You should have created a statement about yourself. Say it everyday. If you haven't written your thank you note, write it now. Clear your mind and heart of the replay of your devalue and start speaking value. Tool number six: the ability to recognize your value through God's eyes; remember that your value was assigned to you before you were born! Psalm 139 says, "All the days ordained for me (and you) were written in Your book before one of them came to be." God has always valued you and has always had a plan for you. He loves you with an extravagant, everlasting love. He is the Good Shepherd who leaves the ninety-nine to find the one. You are the one. He loves you beyond anything you can comprehend. If you still are not sure about this, read the Book of John. See the compassion and heart of Jesus. He values you! To Him, you are prized, precious, splendid, and rare.

Tool number seven: the ability to value yourself and others; to discuss this tool, I want to look at the Book of Esther. The Book of Esther is a unique book. In it, we read of King Xerxes who sent his queen away because he did not like her behavior. He then made a decree that beautiful virgins from all the provinces be brought to the palace. Esther was an orphan who lived with her cousin Mordecai. They were Jews who were exiled during the reign of Nebuchadnezzar. Esther was beautiful and was one of the virgins chosen to go to the palace. Think about what she was facing. She was already an orphan and living in exile, and now she was one of many virgins who, in essence, were kidnapped to be "tested" by the king. After going through 12 months of beauty treatments, each virgin was summoned to a night with the king. This was not their choice. They would enter at night and come out in the morning. Yes, this meant sharing the king's bed against their will. They would enter as virgins and leave to join the concubines, which were sex slaves. Once a girl had been summoned to the king's chambers, she could never marry because she would no longer be a virgin. So now, Esther was an orphan, an exile, held against her will, forced to sleep with the king, and all hopes of marriage and a family were removed. The only "hope" was to be the one chosen by the king to become queen. The king summoned Esther and chose her to be queen. Being queen meant living in the palace and having servants assigned to her, but it did not mean a relationship with the king. Even Queen Esther still had to wait to be summoned before entering the king's presence.

It was revealed to her that the king had issued an edict to "destroy, kill and annihilate all the Jews—young and old, women and children—on a single day…and to plunder their goods." The king did not know that Esther was a Jew. When the plot was revealed, Esther, having been persuaded by her cousin, decided to approach the king without being summoned. She said, "All the king's officials and the people of the royal provinces know that for any man or woman who approaches the king in the inner court without being summoned the king has but one law: that they be put to death unless the king extends the gold scepter to them and spares their lives. But thirty days have passed since I was called to go to the king." Even though she was in danger of being executed, she approached the king. There are many other parts to the story, but in the end, Esther ended up saving the Jews from annihilation.

Why am I telling this story as a conclusion to our discussion of devalue and value? Because Esther took her devaluing situation, she took the wrong, she took the pain, she took the separation from her family, she took the circumstances that she faced, and with God's help, rose above to do something no one else could have done. Her bravery and courage changed lives. Devaluing situations, whether we allowed them or they were forced upon us, can be used for good. I pray that as you have read this book, you have learned how to end devaluing situations, as well as how to heal from devaluing situations of the past. For those of you who have read this book and have not ever been in a devaluing situation, I pray you have recognized what it looks like so you can speak life into those around you who you see in devaluing situations.

You have a king. His name is Jesus. He is the King of kings. He does not treat His people with disdain or use them as

Xerxes did. He loves and cherishes them. You do not have to wait to be summoned into His presence. You can "come boldly to the throne of grace, that (you) may obtain mercy and find grace to help in tome of need." You are a daughter, child of the King.

Let's end by going back to Macy. Macy faced devalue everyday as a small child, yet she found it within her to help those around her who were in pain. Having been devalued, you find yourself in a unique situation to speak life to those who are in the same situation, in a way that no one else can. With understanding and empathy, you can rise above your hurt and your devalue, and help others to do the same. So grab your cherry lip gloss, hold firm to the hand of Jesus, and move forward in value, highly favored child of the King.

CPSIA information can be obtained
at www.ICGtesting.com
Printed in the USA
LVHW040706051020
667929LV00004B/415